Break the silence, tell your truth.

FUTURE VOICES

Edited By Jenni Harrison

First published in Great Britain in 2019 by:

Young Writers
Remus House
Coltsfoot Drive
Peterborough
PE2 9BF
Telephone: 01733 890066
Website: www.youngwriters.co.uk

All Rights Reserved
Book Design by Spencer Hart
© Copyright Contributors 2019
SB ISBN 978-1-78988-613-9
Printed and bound in the UK by BookPrintingUK
Website: www.bookprintinguk.com
YB0407A

FOREWORD

Since 1991 our aim here at Young Writers has been to encourage creativity in children and young adults and to inspire a love of the written word. Each competition is tailored to the relevant age group, hopefully giving each student the inspiration and incentive to create their own piece of creative writing, whether it's a poem or a short story. We truly believe that seeing their work in print gives students a sense of achievement and pride.

For our latest competition *Poetry Escape*, we challenged secondary school students to free their creativity and break through the barriers to express their true thoughts, using poetic techniques as their tools of escape. They had several options to choose from offering either a specific theme or a writing constraint. Alternatively they could forge their own path, because there's no such thing as a dead end where imagination is concerned.

The result is an inspiring anthology full of ideas, hopes, fears and imagination, proving that creativity really does offer escape, in whatever form you need it.

We encourage young writers to express themselves and address topics that matter to them, which sometimes means exploring sensitive or difficult topics. If you have been affected by any issues raised in this book, details on where to find help can be found at: **www.youngwriters.co.uk/support**.

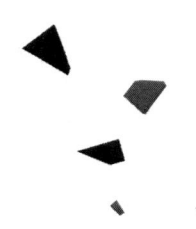

CONTENTS

Independent Entries

Jamie Martin	1
Dess Coleman (15)	2
Ella Mai Leeming (13)	6
Katie Louise Holliday (17)	9
Emma Moore (13)	10
Zahra Kasem (16)	13
Joel Thornton (16)	14
Jessika Kapur	17
Ftoun Abou Kerech	18
Lauren Elizabeth Whitley (14)	20
Dina Sahraoui	22
Sabirin Osoble	24
Shakira Lee (16)	26
Leoni Ward-Walton (14)	29
Jaweria Tariq (16)	30
Joana Kirilova (16)	32
Tom Humphrey	34
Charlotte Marie Patterson (14)	36
Charlie Faulds	38
Kane Stockdale	40
Tessa Mathew (13)	42
Rebekah Zara Murphy (13)	44
Malachai Dauya	46
Amber C S Woodbury (15)	48
Faith Evelyn Cunningham (13)	50
Poppy Snowden	52
Mahrou Meem (14)	54
Amy Rose Bloomfield (13)	57
Julia Galbierczyk (17)	58
George Greiner	60
Kira Nutt (11)	62
Asha Chatterjee (17)	64
Amineh Abou Kerech	66
Ci-Anne Jude	68
Amy Havens (15)	70
Fuad Busoir (18)	72
Kajol Jain (16)	74
Matilda Sophie McCallum Slade (15)	76
Stacey Bates (16)	78
Ifeanyi Giuseppe Ifeji	80
Madalene Howard (14)	82
Maryam Salem (14)	84
Serene Salem (12)	86
Emily Goring	88
Alex Choi	90
Ryan Antony Peddie (14)	92
Emily Alana Helen Hawes (13)	94
Rose Mathew (13)	96
Emma Georgina Phillips (14)	97
Erin Harris (12)	98
Connor Anton Murphy (14)	100
Beth Anderson (15)	101
Deborah Esan	102
Cleopatra Attah (12)	103
Yasameen Rahimi	104
Nancy Gittus	105
Nowshin Ahmed	106
Mekha Benny	107
Nathaniel Ebden (13)	108
Morgan Leah Critchley	109
Amelia Platt	110
Vithoosha Chandirabalan (13)	112
Kainaat Tariq	114
Nifemi Tijani	116
Anna Kanthonga	118
Mollie-Rose Smith	119
Nicholas Nikiforou (12)	120
Maria Aziz	121
Melissa Faith Jones (15)	122

Joseph Lewis Blakeley	124
Emma Skinner (11)	125
India-Rose Marriott (17)	126
Lauren Rose Schofield (15)	127
Ifeoluwa Olusolape Afuwape (17)	128
Judit Climent (17)	129
Dina Samha (12)	130
Amy Turner	131
Elizabeth-Leigh Vogel-Stevens	132
Evelyn Grace Boyd (12)	134
Aysha Mahmood (12)	135
Max Coxon (12)	136
Elizabeth Rose Price (12)	137
Rhys Yeaxlee (14)	138
Macy Ann Hall (17)	139
Fatima Mohiuddin (12)	140
Alfie Fitzgerald	141
Ayomide Adesesan	142
Izzy Goldberg (11)	143
Megan Josephine Swanson (14)	144
Ifeoluwa Ayeni (13)	145
Samia Roshid	146
Sara Syposz	147
Sophia Georgina Verai (12)	148
Sophie Bagley (14)	149
Anna Golding	150
Deanna Watson (15)	151
Madeleine Palash-Weeks	152
Sumaia Rahimi (12)	153
Grace Robinson (13)	154
Aimee Dalby (11)	155
Shenelle Davis	156
Paris Christina Branch	157
Dylan Singh Bains (11)	158
Lewis Paul Healey (12)	159
Skeena Zara Shah (11)	160
Megan Healan (17)	161
Anna Hale	162
Ruth Adetunji (15)	163
Jelani Cecil Eguakun (14)	164
Guinevere Sophronia Edith Fiske (11)	165
Tiyana Lashae Robinson Henriques (18)	166
Emily Jane Carmel Roberts	167

La Vie En Rouge

Red: slick splashes of blood against skin,
a bitter red pool of never fitting in,
beating hearts of those that love in sin
(ironically) praying that love will win.

Red: lashing lava of anger, of rage at
never being able to turn a new page,
never being paid a straight, cis wage,
never being accepted, despite the rage.

Red: secluded shades of non-binary and trans,
always being hit with identity bans,
always seeing more Trump-made plans,
always suffering erasure at political hands.

Red: haunting hues of those oppressed,
stuck in silence, mutely depressed,
invasive questions, never giving rest,
societal bodies forcing more stress.

Red: spectrum of all types of harm,
whether words on tongues or blades on arms,
red are those creeping carefully along a knife,
creeping constantly for a peaceful life.

Jamie Martin

Life And Death

She wore white.
Her presence was no shock to me, I knew she was coming,
Her head was bowed, a hood obscuring her face,
The ends of her dress were wispy and faded,
Floating and waving in the air.
The light around her refracted,
Her head lifted and I could see her face,
Tiny pearls swam in her eyes, occasionally sliding down dark cheeks.
Those eyes were dark,
But they shined like light through honey and candied ginger,
She was smiling at me; a small thing, soft like powdered sugar,
She was not frail or thin, cracked or fractured.
She looked whole.
In one hand she carried a scythe, the platinum blade glinting
And, yet, unthreatening.
Her free hand reached out to hold mine,
Each nail brushed with stardust,
With old galaxies dug under her fingernails.
I looked up into her eyes and a few more pearls, smooth like ocean glass, slipped down her face.
They flicked to something over my shoulder,
I turned to look.

It was... something,
There was something there,
A dark, inky-black thing,
That shifted, swirled and oozed...
It was trying to get closer.
I turned back to Death,
Her face was straining with effort.
Though my throat felt like fractured glass, I opened my mouth.
"What it that?"
Death's voice is soft, low and soothing;
When she talks, it sounds like hushed zephyrs and starlight,
But, then, it was tinged with battery acid and turpentine,
"That is Life," she whispered,
White-noise crept into her voice like fear,
At the confusion on my face, she continued,
"Walk with me, let me tell you a story...
In the beginning, Life and I were balanced,
She was... beautiful.
She made me stars,
Gave me something to compare her eyes to,
Then she made those stars collide and made me gold,
Gave me something to compare her 'heart' to,
She was passion and hope and love,
She was kind,
She made all these beautiful things and gave them to me,
She let them die.

Then, the Earth was created
And, once again, she made me beautiful things:
Flowers, trees, fruit, herbs, spices,
Then fish, and birds and giant creatures,
But the planet, the solar system, was unstable;
Soon, I had to take everything away,
She wasn't angry at first,
But she grew to be.
She fell in love with her creations and thought she could leave me behind.
You, humanity, were the very first thing she created entirely for herself,
You share her passion, her determination
And her desire to create,
But you must all come to me, eventually,
She grew cold, and bitter, and desperate,
Therefore, so did you,
Born into Life that was spiteful
And then you started to take her love away,
You became me and spread to all you could reach,
She never talks to me anymore. It's lonely now."
Death stopped,
Head bowed once more, her hands left mine,
The glow she was emitting dimmed and shuddered
And shrank.
The seething tidal wave of darkness darted forward,
Eager,

Death gasps suddenly, her shaking hands took mine again,
Bright light came from her eyes and she lifted the scythe,
Twirling it expertly but with resignation,
Life slunk backwards and Death smiled a tired smile,
I only just made out what she said next:
"I never meant to hurt you. But I am inevitable.
And you, for most, are but a fleeting second. But not for me, never for me."
Life continued to back away, hesitantly,
Death sighed and opened her arms to me, scythe hovering beside her,
"What happens now?"
"You join me,"
And I did,
I sank into her,
Suddenly, everything exploded,
Cosmic fireworks splattered across my vision
And I was struck by the feeling that I was not alone.
Then it hit me
And all I know is sadness
And peace,
Then there is nothing.

Dess Coleman (15)

My Life

I was born, here, in a working-class town,
A baby full of life and joy,
I was adored by people,
I kind of annoyed people,
Surrounded by family and love,
Growing up is a roller coaster,
Here is my journey so far...

By Year 2 I hated school and I dreaded each day that followed,
I was bullied about looks, isolated and alone,
It all became too much,
I lashed out in anger and caused a girl harm,
That wasn't my intention, it made me really sad
To see that my anger had also made me mad,
I had become a bully, of this I am not proud,
The time had come to make a change and turn my life around.

Halfway through Year 2, we decide that it's time to go,
Time to find another school to help me learn and grow,
This was the best thing we ever did,
Changed me for the better they did!
Made me a kinder, more sophisticated lass,
I was happy in school, kind to my class,
Don't get me wrong, I wasn't a bit dainty!
Even, sometimes I wasn't that brainy.

Move on a year, things begin to go downhill,
My dad's health declines, he gets seriously ill,
I am worried, my dad is in hospital, fighting for his life,
I can't do work, can't focus, can't sleep through the night,
My life is spiralling out of control,
I begin to tell lies and lose friends as I go.

My dad becomes better,
In turn, so am I,
I am enjoying life and the pleasure it brings,
Aced Year 6, came out of the SATs with a perfect score,
Proved to those non-believers that I could achieve so much more.

Year 7 comes along, everything is fine and dandy,
Things become harder, an excuse to push further,
I exceed at my work, get stuck in with it all,
Never was a passenger and never a pilot,
Striving to be the best I can be,
Supporting my peers so we can all achieve.

Things seem lighter, a dim opening in a dark tunnel,
It's shining,
But, oh no!
It's been stolen, taken from my hopeful mind,
The twists and turns of this roller-coaster life,
The darkness returns,
I'm spiralling once more!

Year 8 comes around and things have gotten hard again,
My grandma has dementia, she believes that I am still five,
So many precious memories deleted from her mind,
My heart is breaking, I have forgotten who I am supposed to be,
It makes me question everything, my life, my morality.

I have learnt multiple things through my life that are important,
So important that you need to know and understand,
So, as you are growing up, there's one thing I ask of you,
Hold onto precious moments, never let them go,
Use these as your beacon of light to guide you through to a better tomorrow.

Being different is good,
Don't give a damn about how you look,
Don't listen to the haters,
Be proud to be you.

Ella Mai Leeming (13)

His Poison

She can taste him on her tongue
As gunpowder burns the back of her throat,
As the gravel of her sins strokes the walls of her oesophagus.
The saccharine syrup of his lies coats her teeth
And it stings the cuts in her mouth with viscous mortality,
Merciless.
That is how his passion,
His corruption,
Feels and it tickles the darkest parts of her insides with warm,
Gentle hands.

She can feel the vibrancy of his stare,
The pain of his hands
And the terror of his harrowing words.
They swing in a pendulum of loneliness,
As they slither through the cracks of her heart
And chip away delicately at the locked chambers.
It all accumulates as a thickening fog in her mind,
Makes her heart pound rapidly,
In a soft dance of the rumba.
It all but rocks against her ribs
And cradles her in a soothing hold,
Which helps her to close her eyes
And embrace the static which reverberates under her fingertips.

Katie Louise Holliday (17)

The Human Race

Why did God create this Earth if he knew what it would turn out like?
They say God knows everything, everything,
Past, present and future,
So, I ask you, if he knew about the killing, the arguing and the hatred
That was going to become a part of who we are as a planet,
Why did he bother creating it?

Okay, let's backtrack for a minute.
God.
The master creator of everything.
Knew people were going to suffer and die, yet he still created the Earth and for what?
He knew it wasn't going to change,
He knew about Adam and Eve's betrayal,
He knew about Lucifer stabbing him in the back.
So, again, I ask you, what was the point of creating a universe to watch it stumble and fall?

You're probably wondering where this has all come from, right?
Well, let me start off by saying that everyone is here for a reason.
You are sat there reading this for a reason.
What's my reason for being here?
Well, I'm here to reinstate positivity and perseverance because it seems that people forgot that years ago, it was damaged,

It was broken and hurt by mankind,
I am here to bring it back, make it the trend in your social media feed,
For people to not bring others down, but to hold them up.

On the news lately, there have been some horrifying stories about self-harm and attacks,
Is it just me, or does it make you feel ashamed to be a part of a race which hurt others?
I know we try our best to stop abuse and killings
But did no one ever think to just stop and notice the little kid crying in the street?
When I say abuse and murder, I don't just mean physically.
People get hurt, stabbed from the inside, so much so that they want to do it to themselves for real.

Anyway, back to today's question, any guesses?
Luckily for you, I have an answer.
No, it may not be right but it's all I've got and I believe it is possible,
God knows the future, the past and what you're thinking right now.
He created the Earth because it will be good again,
We will get out of this slump that we call normal and we will do it!
Can't you imagine it?
Walking down the street, breeze blowing and dancing in the sky
As you walk to school, sun shining, impinging on your back,

The neighbours greet you with a friendly wave,
Isn't that a wonderful life?
I believe that we can get there.
All it takes is perseverance and positivity!

You may not have noticed but I said we are a race.
By race, I don't mean black, white, Asian or African,
I mean us.
Us, one and together,
The human race.

Emma Moore (13)

The Ballad Of A Teenager

Distracted from work by the constant pings,
Another beep as my phone sings,
Weary-eyed and dull-tailed,
Awkward and nerdy, proof that I've socially failed.

They walk over me like I'm nothing. A quiet, good
Girl, supposedly transparent and understood,
Their judgment of me, all wrong, they...
They, why does it matter? Who is to say

I'm pretty or smart or good or thin or strong?
Overanalyse a perfect plan and you'll find something wrong,
Stereotypes paint the insides of minds,
Society's view of us is all we find.

What about those who want more? More than
Clothes sizes, make-up colours and fake tans?
Fashion is to express yourself, express yourself,
Not the latest trends, what about our mental health?

The ballad of a teenager, the lasting song,
A society unable to admit that it was wrong
What if I just want to be free?
Why is it so bad just to be me?

Zahra Kasem (16)

Social Media Amnesia

You think that you know me
Because I told you my name,
You tagged me on Twitter,
But I'll never see you again.

Social media amnesia,
I'm forgetting who I am,
How can Silicon Valley
Be changing the thoughts of the land?
They prey on the weak,
The innocent and the lonely,
Or so I've been told,
So, when will somebody be bold?

Silent killer,
Leave your phone beside your bed,
Next thing you know
Your Wi-Fi is the only thing you dread,
420 million have an addiction,
I'm just so sorry
If some of them are your children.

My dad just died,
I posted that,
My grandma's funeral,
I posted that,

A child bullied in school,
I posted that,
Click, click, click
Go the sound of our fingers,
Type, type, snap, snap,
Lemme post that,
Have you seen how good my life is?
I posted that,
But let's not tell them the truth,
(Don't post that.)

Do you realise there are people,
The old,
Cold,
Struggling to breathe?
Their minds ridden,
Bodies frozen,
Lost in their own emotion,
Fighting the flood,
I'd help them if I could,
But why don't you think that we should?
Clicking on their supposedly smart phones?
Swiping left, swiping right,
Monotonous like a machine,
Desperate to find something to like.

We're all so scared,
Suicidal teens

Injected with voices inside their head,
How can you blame them for wanting to be dead?
Menacing adults
Stalking the young,
Why do we give them a platform to perform this act upon?

The government can't stop them,
A petition is never going to contain them,
The world keeps spinning,
But the people have forgotten,
So I guess we have to change the world,
We all need to stop being afraid of ourselves
Because what was once dismal
Can be made beautiful
To cure this social media amnesia.

Silent killer,
Leave your phone beside your bed,
Next thing you know
Your Wi-Fi is the only thing you dread,
420 million have an addiction,
I'm just so sorry
If some of them are your children.

How can you sleep at night
Knowing that there is still a fight?
The world needs to join together
To free themselves
From the social media amnesia.

Joel Thornton (16)

Perfect?

Nobody said life was fair,
The dark mist surrounds us,
There is only so much we can bear,
Yet only a few are actually there to help us.

Some would call it a maze, full of turns for confusion,
Some would wonder where the exit would be,
They would jump to a conclusion
As they fall on their knees, not being able to see.

Success isn't a straight line,
Some may say reach for the stars,
But there isn't only one star, but billions and all shine,
Give it time, and who knows where you would go.

Some are great at science,
Some are great at public speaking,
Some go with the flow,
Some stress themselves more than they can handle.

Nobody is perfect, no matter what you do,
Some try and try, but stars aren't perfect, and neither are you,
Nobody said life was fair,
However nobody said stop trying, nobody is stopping you from being yourself.

Jessika Kapur

My Country Is Bleeding; My Country Is Wounded

I came from the East Gate, from a country full of history,
I came from Jasmine Country and became a dead blossom,
I came from an unfinished childhood and lost my childish face,
A childhood lost moving from city to city to find safety,
A childhood lost moving from country to country to find safety,
A childhood lost moving between continents, Arabia and Europe,
Between old customs and new languages,
I lived in a country that was not my country,
Eid comes and they celebrate and rejoice in their Eid;
I smile, but I do not feel the taste of their feast.
When my grandmother cooked at Eid everyone ate
And we gave food to the poor,
We were watering roses
And smelling the smell of earth with the flowers,
I remember little, little scraps of memories,
I came from a country where something came
To change stars and meteors into Western objects that hurt people,
I came from a country where something came
To change the sound of birds and music to Western voices,
I came from a country where the children have died,
Where the stones have died, where the old men and the trees have died,

Where even the archaeology is lost.
I came from a country where a child is waiting for his father to return,
With tears full of hunger and oppression
And a girl is waiting for her fiance's return,
With tears salty enough to kill the trees.
Where a wife waits for her missing husband to return,
With tears strong enough to dissolve a stone.
Where a mother died of grief over the loss of her martyred son,
Where a mother waits for her son to return with tears that will not dry
And, how sad my heart is seeing older people cry.
I came from a country which poverty, hunger and murder arose to punish.
I wish I could have the childhood that my family and my grandparents inherited,
Their customs, games and memories, all in the same street,
Where the same games are repeated,
I wish I could recount my childhood as my parents recount theirs,
I am sorry to call my childhood premature ageing.

Ftoun Abou Kerech

Words

One day there'll be a time
Where you won't have to hold anything,
You won't have to hold lies, secrets or guilt,
They will fly far, far away from you,
They will leave your consciousness and drown someone else in their weightless heft,
Because words never leave, they will always belong to someone,
That someone might not be you, but you will feel them mocking you twenty-four-seven
To the point where you want to pick out your brain, piece by piece,
Until there's nothing to hear for a while, but they'll come back,
Even if they come in the tone of your voice,
That doesn't mean they're yours,
You know they're not yours because the voice in your head has recited them so many times, you can tell you heard them somewhere before,
But your broken brain can't figure out where, or how, or who said it,
But you know deep inside that you don't own them,
Soon enough, the part of your brain that holds your deepest regrets and fears will take over,
It will possess your lips, teeth and tongue and force you to form words that you can't release,
You vowed to that voice in the back of your head to never speak these things as long as you live,

But you will lose control and they'll spill out like water in an overflowing cup,
You'll be so happy to get those sentences out of your head and into the air,
So happy you'll take a deep breath, so deep your chest begins to burn,
Conducting a tragic symphony in your lungs,
Inhaling all the good in the oxygen around you,
But it will seem like there's no good left
You'll let out all the bad and it will swim around you,
Enclosing you in its darkness,
It'll start to disperse but it will always be near you,
Always one step in front,
It will never leave,
Words tend to do that, stay, whether you wrote them down or said them aloud,
They'll be somewhere, not necessarily near, but close enough.

Lauren Elizabeth Whitley (14)

Home Street Home

I'm not homeless, my home is here...

I don't have a phone
And I don't even have a home,
Living on the streets, day by day,
Memories just won't go away.
What a shame that the life
That once believed in fairy tales and magic
Is now so tragic,
Because I live on the street and I can't stand on my own two feet,
The darkness surrounding me,
And my mind, is making me blind,
She told me there were never any monsters under my bed,
But I now don't have a bed,
So they're all in my head,
I can't get them out,
No matter how loud I shout.
People cry, not because they're weak,
But because they've been strong for too long,
But I just proved all of that wrong.
The government might as well say, "You don't have a home and you're all alone,
And you don't have a bed, so you're not going to be fed,
And I'm not going to give you a piece of bread,
So you might as well be dead..."

I'm human, like everyone else,
But if I had a home
I wouldn't be able to pay my loan!

Right now I'm all alone, sat on the floor,
Crying and begging some more,
But no one seems to care,
They're just acting like I'm not there,
Life just isn't fair!
A penny may seem nothing to you,
But to me, it's a diamond ring,
The things you take for granted,
Someone else is dying for,
Yet you still want more?
This homeless problem needs to be addressed,
I can't carry on in the cold, hardly dressed,
With nothing but a vest on my bare chest,
They get money from the wars,
Yet they can't feed the poor?
So that's why I'm sat on the ground, holding cardboard that says:
'Home Street Home: I'm homeless, not hopeless...'
Help the poor off the floor!

Dina Sahraoui

Am I...

Screaming, they deafened the ears of the white owner,
Instilled with the bravery, defiance and courage, they persisted,
Just because...
Just because my headscarf reflects the modesty within me,
The diamonds studded across me
And, as I rose on the Earth's platform,
They will radiate
And I will say,
This is me.

Am I obliged to go back to my country
Because I am not 'English' enough?
Am I bound to accept that word
Because your favourite rapper spits it?
Am I obligated to accept the stars at my headscarf
As I walk home from school, not knowing,
Not knowing if someone will pull my headscarf off,
Simply for the fact that they're 'scared'?
Not knowing if I'll be attacked for the colour of my skin,
Not knowing if I'll ever stop feeling the relief as I get home safely,
These stereotypes, these racist remarks
Linger in your thoughts, caress your skin
Escape your lips,
Just because...

Just because my tone is rich,
Enriched with the whipping, bleeding
And raping my people have endured,
Infused with the yelling and crying.

Walking outside is a fear
For a young person who owns citizenship in a country,
But is being threatened by bigots whose mind are drunk with beer,
You say we live in a free world,
But then, why are my brothers and sisters being attacked and hurled?
You see, the problem is not the red, white or blue flag
Or your red and white flag,
It is the way that people of that flag carry it and brag,
You claim we steal your jobs,
But, have you ever stopped and realised what is coming out of your gob?

Sabirin Osoble

Let's Talk Mental Health

"Men shouldn't talk about their feelings,"
"You need to man up,"
Those words lingered in the air,
And formed an iron chain around his mouth.

"You're just scared!"
"Grow up!"
Those words fluttered
And barricaded her into a bubble.

"You're fat,"
"Girls are supposed to be skinny,"
Those words were burnt into her skin.

That chain,
It grew,
Weighing him down,
Adding something each day,
Nobody knew,
But what could he do
When he was told
"It's not 'normal' for you"?
With the ability to speak stripped away from him
The pain just increased,
Leaving him to sob and bleed.

That bubble
Distanced her from her use of words,

Her friends, her family, her opportunities,
Feeling faint,
Tensed muscles,
Chest aching,
Numb, sweaty hands,
Shortness of breath,
She went through that pain every day,
But every time a word tried to escape
That bubble reflected it back into her face,
Leaving her eyes leaking
And leaving her with no faith,
But who are we to complain
When we've told her
She's to blame?

Those words,
They changed,
It was stuck in her brain,
Every day she now reads
"Pretty girls don't eat"
She wished her weight to be
As low as her self-esteem,
Vogue magazines,
Weighing scales,
Thigh gaps,
But never mind that,
Because as we know
We were the ones who called her fat.

He can feel,
She can speak,
She can eat
And so can we,
Those seem like basic human natures to me,
So let's just take a step back and meet
To discuss the mental health possibilities
And how we could help each other
If we could just sit down and talk, please.

Shakira Lee (16)

Equality On Earth

I care about equality,
Meaning everyone should get treated the same,
Who are we to decide
If they walk around in shame?

Black, white, yellow or green.
We are all humans inside,
We needed to help solve this problem,
Even great people, like Emmeline Pankhurst, tried.

LGBTQ+ community is a safe place to be,
Which is how it should have started,
Instead of olden day lovers, black, white or gay
Forced to be parted.

Yes, there is some hate against them
Which is what needs to stop,
It's better now than the 'good old days'
When they were always harassed in shops.

I think, personally, some people
Are too hurt or afraid to stand up to help equality,
But different people are the best people
Without having to base it on their sexuality.

Leoni Ward-Walton (14)

Rock-Faced

Solemnized they have become, from the ice-cold winds that etch at their skull,
So much so that one might say they have become one with the wind, blow
Onto their flimsy lives, like paper hearts flowing onto a river, and the dull
Plastic lives they live, soon to be demolished, at sites they try not to show
Any emotion, though it has become hard now.

When rendered were their hearts kept, away in a long wooden box?
Faulty, yet secreting into their lives, like one might pump colour onto a colourless page, so
How far have they come in this undoubted bargaining of their soul? Committed to love, rock,
Like their lives have become pieces of cloth left away in a box for others to sew,
So, now, how do they get out?

Hopeless and agitated like pieces of diamonds left along the shoreside, not knowing their place,
Ashes have flown into the sky and become friendly with the birds soaring high, like
They are not too free, pulled down to the ground amongst the other lifeless statues, who
Told them to be so lonely, left to cry up seas and live lonesome, becoming childlike.

'Til the end, they cry to be opened, to feel their hearts pump against their ears, and
They will do so 'til they die, the to and fro of their consistent lives, day walkers.
Lifeless and blue, how so else should grievers be described?
Tucked away in their own corner, known to be crazy,
They battle with their brain and a person looks toward them,
How depressed must one be to sell off their lives? they think.
But they'll never know.

Jaweria Tariq (16)

Think!

He tells you "Kill!"
And you will,
He tells you "Pray!"
And you obey,
He tells you "Hate!"
You call it fate,
He tells you "Die!"
You go to the sky.

You are thought through fear and fright,
You would always fight.
To escape the rage of your Father,
You would even crucify your mother.
You say you are grateful,
While you are so hateful,
You pretend to love while you shiver,
You are drowning in your holy river.

But through fear you don't learn,
You just escape the fires, the burn.
If I ever ask you "Why?"
What will you reply?
"Because He said so, that's His will."
But is it real?

You don't even own your brain,
It is misty from the rain

Of force-fed words
From violent worlds.
You don't own your heart, your soul,
Because it is noble to be small,
To have no voice, no one to hear,
Only your fear and a shed tear.

You want a saviour, you want a master,
But you are dying in your own disaster.
You like to believe you are led by the light,
But in reality, you are just in fright.
I dare you to open your eyes,
You aren't a bunch of blind mice.
I dare you to think on your own,
I dare you to be grown.

You just want a life in death,
But you are scared of your own breath.
You call it love for Him,
I think your senses are dim,
Because your image of a graceful Lord,
Is to me sadistic, rather cold.
I dare you to know before you believe,
To think before you deceive.

Joana Kirilova (16)

The Blind Eye

Sticks and stones may break my bones,
But words will keep me alone,
Deep, black darkness creeping into my mind,
This deep darkness conquers my brain,
Spiralling out of control,
It's causing me pain,
This bold, black scribble blocking my mind,
But you turned a blind eye.

Your comments and jokes build you up high,
Make you feel powerful,
But they come crashing down on me,
You caused this dark shadow
Cast to destroy,
This small evil crushing me,
Causing all-consuming pain,
But you turned a blind eye.

This dark hurricane tries to destroy me,
Destroy love,
Destroy happiness,
Destroy my family by creating a void to hide me,
Destroy my friendships,
Lonely, but not alone,
But you turn a blind eye.

But, I can't give in to the fear of it,
This storm is just inside my head,
It may feel like my head is being crushed
Or my brain isn't my own,
But I must find a way out,
Seek help,
Will they turn a blind eye?

It's not okay to bully or even make small comments to create pain,
The future needs people to work together,
Care for each other,
Build on love and respect,
It is not okay to beat up, attack or bully people,
Mentally or physically,
It's not okay to ignore those in need,
If you see pain, ask if you can help, if everything is okay,
Tell someone else of your concern,
Give them a route to find help, persuade them to talk,
Be a listening ear,
Do something,
Don't be the one that turns a blind eye.

Tom Humphrey

I Hate That You're Gone

For my dad

I miss you like crazy, I miss you like mad,
But it's so hard to miss someone you know you never had,
Yet, no matter how hard I try, I still really do,
I'll never stop caring and I'll never stop loving you.

They tell me you're still here and you're not really gone,
That you watch over me as my life continues on
And every word I believe for I know it to be true;
You're in my head, my heart and in everything I do!

I wish you weren't gone, I wish you were here
But I know that you're close, I know that you're near
You were taken too early, your life had only just begun
We never got to share any memories or have any fun.

We never got to hug, we never got to laugh
And now all I have is a picture with bubbles from the bath!
We never got to talk, we never got to speak
And now I'm left here alone feeling weak.

Why'd you have to leave, why'd you have to go?
You never got to tell me all that you know.
How can I move on, how can I forget?
I don't even remember us ever having met!

I wish I could tell you I love you more and more each day
That I miss you in every possible way.

Wherever I go, whatever I do,
I'm always left wondering and thinking of you.

Now life passes on whilst you're way up there
And it just isn't right, it just isn't fair!
I hate that you're gone, I hate that you're not here
Even if you are close, even if you are near.

Charlotte Marie Patterson (14)

The Lies We Tell

We lie to each other just as much as we lie to ourselves,
we develop in our own darkening web of lies,
our lies are like our own little fairy tales
that we make ourselves believe,
that we hallucinate to believe because we want to, in fact, need to...
We can't tell the difference between reality and imaginary because we want our lies to become the truth,
the truth we speak in our lies is a desperate cry for help,
we want someone to un-web our coded words,
to see, to hear the real person inside,
the one that keeps banging on the inside doors of their mind,
for someone to notice they're not alright,
for someone to hear them say "I'm fine" and know that's not true,
but no one ever does, mostly because nobody wants to ask since they feel the same feeling,
they know that same face
because every time they look in the mirror that is what they see,
a mask just that, a simple mask
and everyone's too scared to shout out or ask for help
because that's who we are,
we're humans...
We feel human emotions and yet we don't like to admit that,

so even though they don't like or want to, they'll wear their masks
because everyone else does,
they think it's normal so they'll be 'normal'
but for how long?
How long will their masks last until it breaks
and we see everyone's true emotions?
What happens then?

Charlie Faulds

Outside

Outside is like an unknown roller coaster,
You don't know what it is or if it's as it appeared on a poster,
You don't know for sure that it's safe,
If it goes slow or it will gradually increase the pace.

You don't know who's on the roller coaster,
A girl you like or a guy who always gets closer,
The more paranoid you get, the closer he gets,
Then he takes your place and leaves you in the mess.

The mess is where he came from,
He wanted you to be in a mess where it leaves you numb,
You were all lucky and happy,
But you never thought about how you were so lucky and happy.

You only came to realise how lucky you were
When that guy came and left you bare,
That mess you're stuck in,
You don't wanna be there forever duckin'.

You can only get yourself out, no other,
Come to realise you're not the same as each other,
Living the high, happy and dandy,
But never thought about getting in this situation, that would have been handy.

When you get up out of the mess, you're gonna take your place again,
Can't say nothing yet, it's a matter of when,
Take your time, go at your own speed,
Go when your guts have settled and take what you need,

When that spot in life is taken back
You will realise no one will notice anything that you lack,
Everything is back to normal, the way it was,
Now next time you know what to do and what is the loss.

Kane Stockdale

My People

I look around the bus station, on a cold winter day
And I see everlasting white,
These people were beautiful,
The paleness of their skin seemed like such a contrast
To the muddy and earthy tone of my skin.
Here I stuck out like a sore thumb,
I may know their language, their way of thinking
And share their thoughts,
But I still wasn't one of them, the odd one out.

I catch my bus and travel to a different place,
Searching for my people, my home.
I reached a different destination.
It wasn't a cold winter night here, it was a warm sunny day,
Here I looked out to see people with sun-kissed skin and melanin,
These people were beautiful,
Here I was just like all of them,
One of many.
Until I opened my mouth.
All around me, people spoke in different voices and a different language,
But when I tried to copy them, all that came out was a mumbled jumble of uncertainty,
Once again, the odd one out.

Defeated, I caught another bus,
I came to the conclusion, that I had no people and no home,
I was just way too different.
I caught another bus, far, far away from these places
And I met many other people just like me,
Brown skin, but another voice
And I realised they were 'my people'
And they were beautiful.

Tessa Mathew (13)

A Picture-Perfect Phoney Princess

Imagine shopping in a shop that's specifically for you!
Imagine owning more money than you know what to do!
Imagine uploading a picture fabricated with Photoshop,
Imagine people looking up to something that's a flop!

Well, fit for the fraudulent and fictitious female ruler,
Empowered by feminism that's specified to a size 6,
Certain ethnics, edited and full of graphics,
How do we look up to something so plastic?

Fake this and fake that,
"Oh, did you hear about how this non-fat?"
Sponsorships make her rich
How do we know that they don't give her an itch?

She created a beauty line
And got so much income it could pay for her new neckline!
A perfume bottle not fit for a child
Her most loyal followers
And it wasn't that mild.

You'll see them on the catwalk of your favourite brand,
Inducing you into a false state of mind.
"Go buy that product!" that brand said
So you got the product and ended up wearing it to bed!

In a world full of diversity
How are we so blind that we don't see our true beauty that's booming inside?

So, go on ahead, like her post,
Buy her brand
But remember...
You're the one that's paying for her next holiday; coast to coast.

Rebekah Zara Murphy (13)

War Horse

Laughing, joking, smiling,
The young soldiers joined the forces,
Started their journey overseas
And taking with them their horses.

Walking, running, skipping,
Our troops travelled miles and miles,
They didn't know what they were into
Because when they got there, it was vile.

Filthy, dirty, disgusting,
The trenches made the youngsters start crying,
Eventually, they were forced upon the battlefield
And the propaganda cheated them into dying.

Loading, aiming, firing,
The soldiers stole each other's lives,
And everyone in their homes were mourning
Parents, children and wives.

Starving, aching, resilient,
There was rationing at home and in the trench,
The food was scarce and disgusting
For the English, German and French.

Working, farming, welding,
The women at home didn't stop,

They made ammunition and uniform
And did their best to harvest the crops.

Singing, writing, learning,
We have many ways to remember the dead,
Our main symbol that we use is the poppy
Black and bloody red.

Brave, courageous, gallant,
We are in the soldier's debt,
We will remember the soldiers
We will never forget.

Malachai Dauya

Be Yourself

Everything you think I am is far from the truth,
The way I portray myself to be normal, to blend in, but what is normal?
How do you blend in?
People laugh around you and you feel like it's at you,
You're in your own deflating bubble with the muffled sounds around you,
This isn't something you can just return at a store,
Walk past on a shelf and be like, no thank you!
You took years away from my life that I cannot get back,
I am not a bear you can poke with a stick
Or a bull you can hurt just for fun,
I'm walking away from the old me, escaping the toxic moments in my life,
I want to be me, who I really am!
I fell down but I got right back up,
I'm not the only kid who grew up like this, we empty ourselves so we feel nothing,
It's like constantly looking into a broken mirror, with our face deformed like people think we are
And standing there wondering what it would be like if that mirror was fixed,
If we were understood,
I'm not who you want me to be, you've controlled me for too long!
I want to be free, I want to be me!
Who I really am!

I want to be loved without the constant stares,
I want to feel safe and stood by.
Not on my own even though I know I'm not.
I want to be me!
I am me!

Amber C S Woodbury (15)

The Cycle Of Poverty

Clouds of dust rise from the sweltering pavement,
As my bare, sore feet slap harshly down,
Ebony legs bounding forward,
Breaking into a sprint,
Ligaments, tendons, joints bursting,
The radiant sun observes
The distant ash-green mountains overlook,
Yet, my deep brown eyes shine like an ackee seed,
I will not stop.

Through the sea of swimming faces
The congested road is bleached with heat,
Rows and rows of saturated, colourful shacks,
Packed close together, paint worn and flaking,
Washing lines strewn from ancient electricity poles
Hang ragged, faded clothes like bunting,
Although the rhythmic reggae tunes play
And the rust-zinc fences weather,
I must go on,
So I run a little faster,
Skeletal arms pumping,
Lungs burning, a fire roars deep in my chest,
Throat parched,
Skin drenched in sweat,
Red-hot veins throbbing in my temples,

Salty tears whipped away by the air resistance,
I stop.

Head spinning, I look up,
The doorstep crumbles beneath where I sit
In the mud, amongst debris and littered junk,
The repetitive reggae beat drives me insane,
A plump black woman braids intricate patterns into my scalp,
The sun mocks me, its everlasting blaze,
There's no escape,
A bitter tear runs down my cheek,
No matter how hard I run, the cycle continues.
The cycle of poverty.

Faith Evelyn Cunningham (13)

Content

Walking away never seemed so easy before,
Between the tentative touch of a lover's hand
And the cold scar of loss that made me a wandering stranger
On a faraway shore,
A better version of myself seemed like a vile complex,

Until...
The glistening sunlight of the pensive day
Left my mind raw
And my conscience hopeful.

However,
The cold, complicated cage
Of a modern, misguided society still haunted me,
The uncomfortable perspiration of a controlling conservative structure
Left little room for a simple existence,
For me to simply
Be.

This beautifully open reconstruction of my mind
Felt I didn't have to be this creative, being for the masses,
But it was dampened by the harsh clouds of my worries
And my every day coaxing me from around the bend in the road.

I cower,
I fear it,
I am not content,
I trudge through the weighty lament,
I drown in the tasks
Until I am lifted up from my lying mask
Into something more fulfilling.

The thought that I could be content
Among the dismal and grey that torments
Was a soul-altering thing,
Rocketing me back to the sadness of last spring.

It doesn't bother me anymore,
For my mistakes mean little, so, thus I close this door,
Walking out along the moor,
Standing on the hill I did yesterday,
But I am different,
I am content.

Poppy Snowden

Sheep

Tinted windows,
Broken glass,
You see them clearly,
You let them pass.
You hold them tight,
You keep them safe.
You should know
You're their only faith.
The thorns, they grow
Along the stem,
Riding up,
To the poisonous gem.
Stab by stab,
Little by little,
Their swords get deeper
And your words become fickle.

The hold in your voice,
It begins to waver.
The taste of your strength
Loses its flavour.
But their eyes still gleam
To get a glimpse,
Their mouths still water
To get a kiss.
Once they've ravaged,

They lick their lips,
Once you're ruined,
They lose their grip.

They have a cloth around their eyes,
You have wound them shut.
They have a cloth around their mouths,
You have bound them tight.
But still, they follow,
Still, they weep,
For the tiny scraps
That lie at your feet.
And, you begin to wonder,
Will they dare?
Will they hunt,
Steal,
Beat,
Kill?
Will they care?

Though they cannot see,
They follow you blindly,
Though they cannot speak,
They hum your praises mutely
And though they are dumb,
Lame and obsessed,
They become your worth,
They fill your chest.

Where others have gold,
You have your sheep
That lie and cry,
Their labour cheap.
Where others have fame,
You have your sheep,
That break every rule,
Every bond they reap.

Mahrou Meem (14)

The Teenage Mind

A little broken,
that's what we are,
what we feel cannot be spoken
and what we do can't be explained.

We don't tell you that living is such a pain,
being happy is a treasure that can't be gained,
we care so much about how we look,
when all we want is a weight to be lifted off.

We all think we're overweight,
when not a pound has been obtained,
we just want to not feel afraid
and for everything to not be overthought.

We try not to cry because that's weak,
so, we express ourselves with anger and hate,
we don't mean anything we say,
because our minds are too bleak.

Though it may not seem that we want your help,
it's because our screams are muted,
I swear, we really do want to be kind,
that's a place where we need assistance,
but, for now, we hope you enjoyed this small insight,
to the teenage mind.

Amy Rose Bloomfield (13)

Ode To My Dreams

I make a promise to seek that what truly counts,
I make a promise to reach out to the stars,
I'm fighting a dark war within,
I'll make it out, I'll reach my goals, I'm going to win!

Everything happens according to our clock, our time,
We all can reach our dreams, just maybe not right now,
Start with a small step, make it a big priority,
It's essential to change your reality.

You'll hear my name, you'll hear my voice,
You'll see me standing tall,
I make a promise, I'll find my purpose, I'll reach my goals,
I will be happy, I will stay strong,
I will live my dream life, where I belong.

I make a promise to build myself up again,
I make a promise to fight through all the pain,
I may be lost, tired, lacking confidence,
But I'm not finished, I'll keep fighting,
My dreams will come true one day.

I keep my eyes on the prize, even when it's too dark to see,
Because soon I'll rise, become stronger, become free,
Free from all these overwhelming thoughts, the anxiety,
Free to make my dreams become my reality.

This is my promise, the ode to my dreams,
But also, my warning too,
Dear obstacles in my life, watch out!
I'm coming for you.

Julia Galbierczyk (17)

What A Waste Of A Bath!

I was having a wash,
Sat in my tub,
When my stomach began to grumble,
Fancying some grub,
I looked at the time,
I'd only been in ten minutes,
What a waste of a bath.

I sat and pictured,
A delicious meal,
My mouth watered at the thought,
I got out of the water,
To make this thought real,
What a waste of a bath!

I grabbed up a towel,
And rushed to the kitchen,
I got out some lamb,
And don't forget the bread!
I picked up some butter,
And began to spread,
Yet the whole time I was thinking the same thing,
What a waste of a bath...

I finished my sandwich,
And washed up my dish,
I noticed how quick I was,

And thought, *I might make it!*
But in the back of my mind, a thought still nagged,
What a waste of a bath!

I traipsed back up the stairs,
Before I noticed,
The water behind me had left a path,
I returned to the kitchen and wiped it all up,
Before heading for the tub,
And in my head, I was thinking, yet again,
What a waste of a bath.

I walked into the bathroom,
I unravelled the towel,
Before dipping a toe into the suds,
The water was ice-cold,
What a waste of a bath!

George Greiner

Swimming Life

First morning light
After a restful, dark night,
Up before dawn,
All I do is yawn and yawn.

Facing two hours of training,
Whilst outside, it's raining,
Warming up, stretching my body,
This will always be my favourite hobby.

This is the day, the day I race,
I assure myself I'll pick up my pace,
Waiting with anticipation at the block,
I will now be racing against the clock.

Butterflies I feel, waiting for the whistle to blow,
Take your marks... Go!
I'm pounding through the water, my heart feels loud,
Listening to the roar from the excited crowd.

I'm sprinting to the wall,
I'm giving it my all,
At every breath, I'm gasping for air,
I put everything into this, I really care.

I have stopped the timing pad,
I feel exhausted but I am so glad,

Glancing at the leaderboard, my breath I hold...
I have just realised I have won gold!

I gave my blood, sweat and tears,
I faced my greatest fears,
My training was immense,
Now, it's all making sense.

Kira Nutt (11)

Lies, Damn Lies And Cosmetics

Wine-red lips, radiant skin,
irresistibly attractive siren,
people say you're shallow and superficial, not even skin deep,
but you're always there when I need you.
My shadow, my selfie confidante, my best friend,
you help me fit in and stand out,
you're my social camouflage and my fanfare.
You keep my secrets and hide my scars,
you maintain my facade,
tell my version of the story,
humour my vanity.
You build my confidence and poise,
you brighten my eyes and exaggerate my smile.
On dark days, you keep people out of my way,
my tears slice through you like a shard through silk,
but you fix me.
You're my fix.

I want to be Photoshop-perfect,
an unforgettable image,
timeless and flawless, like the marble complexion of Aphrodite,
heads must turn in validation.
Whispered approvals and jealous glances amplify my self-esteem.
Mirror, mirror on the wall,

I'm the fairest of them all.
No midnight Cinderella, I'll stay a butterfly forever,
all beauty, no beast,
pretty and playful,
painted, not tainted,
self-expression, not narcissism,
a polished truth, not a lie.
Well... maybe a white lie.
All made-up.

Asha Chatterjee (17)

Days Pass But The Past Does Not Move

Days pass, but the past does not move
The first tent is the first day
And the last night.
First tent under the rain
And among the flowers.

I remembered my homeland,
I remembered the flowers
When I was first planted,
How I waited day after day
To grow among the grasses.

There was a lake close to the tent
The colour of the water was black
And in the depths were green algae
And insects that sank into the water.

I remembered the children
When they sank into the wide sea,
They screamed their loudest,
They screamed and said "Mama!"
They shouted and said, "Sea, O Ghaddar!"

There was a grove close to the tent,
I walked on the stones and counted
Each step I took.

I was afraid of any tiny shock.
I was laughing,
But my heart trembled

I remembered when I saw
Houses and orchards destroyed
In front of my eyes.
I saw spirits flying
Into sky and bodies flooded with dust.

Days pass, but the past does not move.

Amineh Abou Kerech

Knife And Its Crime

Knife,
An instrument that cuts through an object,
And crime,
Breaking the law,
But why?
Why on Earth do we have to pick up a knife
And take an innocent life?
And, why?
Why do we need to wake up to the toxic news that a boy aged fourteen is stabbed to death?
He's dead, his family emotionally dead, children dead, and young successful adults-to-be dead,
Just cos of the glamorous watches they wear!
Can't you see, it's not yours to wear?
But I doubt *you* care.
I know this question might seem kind of deep.
But is the Devil inside you?
If you want to kill, steal and destroy
An innocent's life
The Devil must be in you, but he can leave you
If you find something more constructive to do,
Help the families of the traumatized and terrified,
Help those in custody that picked up a knife,
Join local youth clubs and make one too,
Help the police force,
The paramedics too,

Those people who bring justice to those crippled in fear,
I'm speaking the truth and stating the facts
Knife crime is rising
And London needs its youth,
So stop fighting
And let's start resolving.
#stoptheknifecrime

Ci-Anne Jude

In Harmony

I wanna be one of the cool girls,
the pretty girls,
the perfect ones.

I wanna mess around with the fun guys,
the jokes, laughs, finger-guns.

I wanna be the rebel, the scary one
black hair, big eyes, red lips.

I wanna be the weird ones,
who don't care for the stares,
with girls and guys on their hips.

I wanna be the clever ones, the nerds, the sweats,
or the carefree ones
who float about.

But I can't 'cause I'm not in the movies,
the stereotypes are real but the friends aren't.
so I blank out.

Ignore the looks, the judge in her expensive
trainers and face without the breakouts.
she looks down on me grinning, 'cause
she isn't left behind.

I have to keep going, keep turning the tedious
cogs of life, just to give me peace of mind.

I must fit in somewhere but that somewhere
is getting harder and harder to find.

I grab out, grasping to find someone to
cling onto, to make memories, play the part,
but when I take off the filters, I'm blind.

Maybe I'm wrong, too different
too smitten.

Still stuck in my stupid little hole
and the only way out is to fit in.

Amy Havens (15)

Floating

Floating.
In a pool of your own blood,
Your soul heaves its last sigh,
Life pours out of the gaping hole in your chest,
Next to the spot your mum always kissed when you were a baby.

Another young man was stabbed in London today.

You won't live long enough to learn that you're famous,
Won't live long enough to find your first love,
Won't live long enough to start a family,
Won't live long enough to live.

The streets will finally know your name.
For a while.
You fought for this,
Worked for this, laid down your life for this,
But now it's all over.
You just lie there.

Floating.
In a pool of your own mistakes,
No more fighting, no more working,
No more living, nothing to do but float.
Is this what Heaven feels like?
The sky looks bigger than the biggest ocean.
You can't wait to float in it.

But the medic keeps blocking your view.
He's saying something.
What?
It doesn't matter.
You just lie there.
Floating.

You live by the knife,
You die by the knife.
Young kings,
It is not your time to float yet.

Fuad Busoir (18)

A Cry For Help

Caged, yet free,
What an odd home of old plastic bottles
And sludge in their once clear water surrounding them,
Sharp ends on the sands,
One wrong move and...
It's over.
Rays reflecting off the metal bottle-tops,
Their quiet pleas echo as they reach out desperately,
But no one hears a sound,
They mourn in silence,
A lone pigeon stumbles, a thin wire tangles,
Pulling its foot tighter
And tighter,
Their indignant squawks, a cry for help,
Once free, they yearn to roam free once again, they seek
Freedom from their predator,
Freedom from us,
Unheard, or rather ignored
By the selfish individuals that abuse them,
Tumultuous sounds as they quarrel with one another,
Yet, they seek comfort in their shared suffering,
What are they, mobile machines for entertainment, tossed around?
Their pounding heartbeats,
All they desire is liberation from the world,
Why don't we

Free them from captivity,
Free them from their misery?
Kajol Jain (16)

No One Understands

There's a demon in my head,
But he answers to my name,
He tells me stories when I'm in bed,
The thoughts confuse my brain,
When I go to leave the house,
The thoughts cause me pain,
Laughing at my frustration,
Not understanding the irritation,
Doctors just giving an estimation,
Until they reach the final destination.

Worrying all the time,
A mentally-drained teenager,
I'm as green as a lime,
It's a sick feeling,
That's the anxiety train,
Constant fear,
Constant pain,
I speak to my peer,
No one to listen,
The horror glistens,
No one helps.
Yes, I am struggling,
The voice in my head has my thoughts bubbling.

I need help,
I need someone to break the belt,

The one that's making me yelp,
I want the thoughts banned,
I should have this all in hand,
I will never win,
Keeping this all in, I'll never win.

Matilda Sophie McCallum Slade (15)

Bleeding Star

Burning slowly, burning bright,
Lost in darkness, lost at night,
All alone, no one cares,
No one asks, no one dares.

Far away, but still so near,
In dark, in night, it shines so clear,
But beneath the light, there's nothing there,
Deepest secrets too hard to share.

The chaos, the hurt, no one sees,
Timid voice, begging "Please..."
A simple act can end it all,
Fade to black, choose to fall.

Consuming pain, it's all too much,
That burning light, too hot to touch,
With a pill or blade or gun
The light will fade and all is done.

Now the dark has lost its light
And the lone star has lost her fight,
The others cry and shout and scream,
Too caught up in their blissful dream.

Now, they feel all the pain,
All the guilt and all the shame,

They laughed and teased and ignored the star,
Now they know, they went too far,
So, in the dark and lonely night,
The flicker, shimmer, slightest light,
The little star had joined the sky
She grew her wings and learned to fly.

Stacey Bates (16)

Reverie

He looks on to the window,
An interesting thing for his eyes to see,
A call to start his reverie,

A tree, bearing dreamlike fruits

Each branch free to grow wherever it pleases,
Flowering in the wind breezes,

Unfortunately, then does he see that
He can also relate to these
Branches, swaying in a wind out of their control,
Born from a common root,
All dreams the same, all constrained by all,
Like him, manufactured to be obedient,
A human medium of exchange,
Human capital.

Then the slothful pavane dance of the snow,
Swallowed by the confines of the window

Is lost to the classmate
As he is broken from his reverie,
He looks on
As his classmates uniformly behold and "Whoa"
Whilst he is planted in the third row,
Part of a scholastic tree
And so it goes on, trapped in this monotony.

Wings clipped, aquiline eyes straying to see past the cage,
There is an interesting thing for his eyes to see,

A call to start again his reverie.

Ifeanyi Giuseppe Ifeji

Sweet Woodlouse

Your wind-whistled back,
Curves with each tad of
Gentleness,
Lapsing,
In,
Out,
Like tedious tides
Below the glorified moonlight,
Forever waxing,
Waning
And then,
Eclipse.

Where are you?
You have a tendency to
Scuttle and burrow
Under the damp heartbeats of
Autumn,
A collage of withered souls,
A camouflage of reds, yellows and brown
Ruffled amongst rounded gems of crispness
And...
There you are,
Nestled in the basking saffron sunlight,
Your skeletal structure and fading greyness,
Your ribbed back and panned brown,

Your delicate legs, an array of pitter-patters
Like the rain bombarding your environment,
Parcels of succulent drops from the heavens above.

Or, like ballet dancers
On pointe,
You crawl over my hand,
You are a spectacle,
Then you spindle off
Into your cranny
Of wet wood,
Clammy yet cosy
And teeming with life,
Satisfied with your day's work
You curl up
And now rest,
Safely,
Sweet woodlouse.

Madalene Howard (14)

What They Say (Or Don't)

In school, I ask a question,
They never seem to hear,
I keep it hidden,
I don't hold it to them,
They just didn't hear, I know,
I was just too quiet.

But I wish they had heard,
I still cry over it and imagine what could have been,
I just don't let them see
It's still painful,
I just wish I did not care.

But when they do hear
I have to watch my tongue,
I never know what's going on
So anything I say could be wrong.

On social media they say
Who are you?
What's your name?
And what on Earth did you just say?
I didn't mean to offend,
I was trying to be nice.

So next time I am around,
Please take care,
I have fragile emotions

And I really care,
When you don't hear
I just don't want to ruin your day.

And I'm sorry I sounded mean
I didn't mean to be rude,
I didn't know it would bother you,
Would you even believe
I might have been trying to be nice?

Maryam Salem (14)

In The Courtroom

In the courtroom -
I am the Truth, accused and abused.

The judge comes in,
Crushing every grain of hope under his bulldozer strides,
Justice, they say, is served between these four walls,
But, how can this be when...
The judge before me speaks words
Shrouded in a fur of foul-tonged lies?
His eyes unsee egregious evildoing,
His mind is replete
With the venom of vile misguidance,
This judge's honour is false,
His rank, betrayed.
His very presence
Turns the throne of justice
Into a worm-eaten, rickety stool.
Around me I see
The sun's rays of sincerity,
Blocked out by the blinds of deceit
And shrivelling saplings of revolution
Are deprived of the water of courage.
Deep, deep within...
The court's very heart
Beats with the blood of betrayal,
Pulsing through its veins,

I am the Truth, accused and abused.
But I will rise.
I will speak.
And I will...

Break free.

I am the Truth.

Serene Salem (12)

Sunflowers Are Safer Than A Rose

Toxic and cold your mind lay
suffocated with irrelevant triggers,
engulfed with numerous attempts to free you
from your isolated abyss,
simple action, drastic effect
can I not help?

But I've realised
I did not obtain the thorns
that drove me to insanity or
weighed us down to the depths
of the deep blue below
and it was not my mind corrupted
with constant anxiousness and jealousy,
but it was yours.

Your thorns weighed us down
and suffocated my heart with a constant routine,
your thorns that are sinking swiftly
towards the core of us,
the beautifully scarred core of us
but we cannot be fixed, we are
beautiful battered souls
and your thorns have sunk too deep.

So, I must rip them out now my love,
it may hurt for a second, but, I can assure you

after the pain has settled
and your eyes dry,
you are free to wander,
but I blame myself, after all
sunflowers are safer than a rose.

Emily Goring

Wolves

Silent as the night, the delicate wolves
Carefully travelled through the plain forest,
Seldom was there a moment
Where the wolves were spotted resting,
Even as the incoming darkness covered
Up the sun like a closing blind.

The wolves were still restless.
Near to the spot where the wolves were,
There was a human camp,
As the wolves drew on, the
Dogs of human property,
Started whimpering.

This alerted the humans, but the
Wolves drew nearer to the dogs.

Bang!
The clear shot rang through
The silent night
And struck home.

A shaggy wolf collapsed to the
Ground, and the pack scattered.

For the forest, they ran.
Bang!

Another shot rang out and a wolf collapsed
To the ground.

The wolves ran and ran,
Until the sound of the shots were distant,
Finally, the terrifying sound ceased
And the wolves
Collapsed to the ground, exhausted
And
Lay there
For the night.

Alex Choi

Thinking

Love,
What an emotion,
Some say it'll bring the best out of you,
But I drink my water
And say,
It did nothing but destroy me.

Some say,
Oh, you'll be so happy when you find it,
They didn't mention
That was just a temporary thing.

I could say
That yes, love was amazing,
But then, what did I feel after a relationship?
Because surely a heartbreak
Is love trying to grow
When it's being confined?

Believe it or not,
Heartbreaks really kill
And, if it's love,
Then why do we say it's so perfect?

We lie,
Telling kids that love is inevitable and everlasting
When it isn't,

Or, not in a good way anyway,
Surely we can't let kids break themselves?

Because, guess what?
Love destroys you,
Stomps you,
Makes you the ground.

And so I rest what I have said,
I sip my tea
And wonder,
What is love?
Nothing but an inevitable curse.

Ryan Antony Peddie (14)

I Am Not Good Enough

It's hard to feel good in a world of bad,
With others trying to get you down.
It feels like they're out to get you
And drag you to the ground.

It seems like you're okay,
But you're really crying inside,
You feel like you're not good enough,
When the truth is, you really are.

Your friends find new people,
Leaving you in the dark.
I'm not good enough, you think to yourself,
Those thoughts define who you are.

These thoughts stop you from trying,
From trying to follow your dreams.
Doubt drowns encouragement
And you believe all the bad.

What you need is people who really care,
People who make you feel wanted.
They tell you that you are better
Than you could ever believe.

The one thing you need to lift your spirits,
Is not money or fame,

The one who makes you feel respected,
Is a true, caring friend.

Emily Alana Helen Hawes (13)

In Their Homes

In her home, the silence in the living room is deafening,
She remembers the Christmas music that came out of
the radio,
Only one year ago.
In his home,
The loneliness in the hall is frightening,
He remembers the racket of children waiting to sing 'Happy Birthday' to him,
Only one year ago.
In her home,
The sights in the garden are horrifying
As she remembers the times when all was just fun
and games,
Only one year ago.
In his home,
The pain in the kitchen is terrifying
As he remembers the different smells of curry so lovingly made by his mother,
Only one year ago.
So when I think about peace,
I think of this boy and girl coming back to a home where there is laughter, cuddling and moments of feeling good about all that is around.

Rose Mathew (13)

Red Runs Red

Light and dark,
Black and white,
Colours in a representational spectrum,
Illuminating the symbol of life,
A social cancer of pain and hurt,
Twisting, turning,
Falling, burning,
An intertwining river of social conduct,
Multiplied by those who support the fight,
To save a life,
A skeleton of dignity,
Outlining the values of our modern world,
A divided culture, light and dark,
Ripping and splitting the world apart,
Yet, together, red runs red,
The blood of harmony forever shed,
In matrimony of its scarlet colour,
Brings blackened hope upon each other,
Together, we rise,
To outlast those who bleed the wrong,
Together, we rise,
A society strong,
Harmony absorbing the division of colour,
To create a world where we fight for each other,
Through hearts of hope, not stories of skin,
We will outlast this destroying sin.

Emma Georgina Phillips (14)

The Victim

I stand there in the playground,
Wondering where to go,
Nowhere is safe now,
Your hatred has stooped too low.

Not looking back,
I run and hide,
Finally finding some cover,
Whilst my heart beats inside.

Your words fire at me,
Like a knife through the heart,
It's been going on for so long now
That I can't remember the start.

Your fists are a boulder,
That torment me all the time,
Is it too late now
To stop this awful crime?

Trying to pluck up the courage
To tell my teacher the truth,
To show her all my bruises
And my beaten, wobbly tooth.

I'm going to tell my teacher,
Tell her what's not right,

Hopefully, it will fix things,
Stop this continuous fight.

When she calls you into the office,
When she calls your name,
Please, can you be truthful?
Don't pretend it was just a game.

Erin Harris (12)

Taekwondo

I respect Taekwondo,
The rules of a good fight you know,
Just like tying my shoes,
When I go, I know what to do,
I've done Taekwondo for eight years,
I've had to face all my fears,
I've had blood and tears
And faced some hard competitors,
I've gone from white to black belt,
Some people mess and teachers yell,
I'm going for my second dan soon,
I'll keep coming back, like a dog getting a groom,
I can't wait to get my ninth dan
No Premier Inn needed, just a caravan,
I remember the time I was pushed to my limit,
All the other times, I would usually win it,
I am now top of my class,
I am glad I got my A grade pass!
I now teach all the new kids what to do,
Every week I come back and ask, "Who are you?"

Connor Anton Murphy (14)

River

You ask who I idolize, but at first, I thought the topic was quite controversial,
Perhaps I idolize the moon, who basks in her own glory,
Everyone is familiarised with her elegant light that births a whole new world beneath her,
Because when the sun leaves, she is the nightly ruler.
Or, perhaps, I idolize the sun,
For he is essential for life and he is the opportunities of a new day,
But I realize now, above all, I am my own idol,
I am stuck with myself,
But not in the way a bird is trapped in a cage,
I am stuck with myself in the way a marital vow has joined two passionate lovers,
Lovers who are meant to be together.
I am my own hero because, despite everything,
I have always been my own motivator and strength to overcome life's obstacles.

Beth Anderson (15)

Friendship

It says in the Bible, 'Bad company corrupts good morals',
So don't expect there not be quarrels,
I plead with you try to talk to your peers
Because they will listen to your fears,
Regardless of what they hear.

Proverbs 18:24
There are 'friends' who destroy each other,
But a real friend sticks closer than a brother,
So let us aspire to be supportive of one another,
Even if we do not come from the same mother.

Now, a feeling of trust is defined as hope
And without it, do you really cope?
Aspire to help others and always be humble,
Because those same people will help you when you stumble.

So, I ask you, what is a friend?
A friend is someone who always has a hand to lend.
A friend is someone who is there for you in your time of sadness,
Someone who changes your sorrow into gladness.

Deborah Esan

Us... Just Us

When I look around me, I can see
What the world was made to be,
A wonderful place of diversity
Where we attack every adversity,
It breaks my heart to see others
Comparing their skin to one another's,
Just like me, be proud of your skin,
Don't put yourself in a place I've been,
Where you put yourself down
And lose your crown,
Because when I look at you
I wish they knew
What a beautiful soul you are.

Many times, they hated me,
But look at who I've come out to be,
When I leave my bed
I go ahead
And take on my new role,
I become Superwoman because that's the goal,
I dream to be strong and independent,
Brave and ultra transcendent,
I love all my attributes,
From my hair down to my boots
And I hope you do the same,
But if you don't that'd be a shame.

Cleopatra Attah (12)

Stuck

Too many choices in the wrong direction,
Only just for protection,
I see the picture of suffering like it's a collection,
Too many wrong choices in the wrong direction.

Breathe.
That's what I was told to do.
I close my eyes and I see their faces,
The pressure is on.
My hands tremble as I pick up the pen,
My mind going blank like a piece of paper,
Everything I have done has gone to waste,
I can't ask for help without feeling ashamed.
I can't get the words out of my mouth.
Breathe.

I felt like a bird with a broken wing
Trapped in a cage.

Look at me now, not envious nor hateful,
But with love and pride
Because that's all I deserve.
I have learnt to love myself and accept who I am,
So look at me now and tell me what you see.

Yasameen Rahimi

The Field Of Red

The sun, rising cold in morning skies,
Little it cares, for little it knows.
The treachery, carnage, rebellion,
The people, strewn and littered, as if they had been simply tossed away, by a carefree breeze.

Even the devil can't imagine the hell up here,
Blood turns fields red,
Tears turn rivers to seas,
Pain turns a soldier's heart.
All emotions gone but hate.

As the sun rises, it sees
Beautiful carnage,
The perfume of rotting,
A cowardly man, who died for his country,
A lone soldier stranded, no way out,
No way home,
A scream fills the trees,
All he can do is wait
For death.

This is what I see now.
This is what I think now.
Every time.
The field full of rotting corpses, fighting for their home.

Nancy Gittus

The Inevitable

I woke up miserably,
Told my mum that I was sick,
Pretended to vomit. *Ick! Ick! Ick!*
My brother came and took the mick.

I had to go to school
No ifs or buts.
First off food tech, the teacher was nuts,
Next in maths, thrown by a plethora of sums,
In English, we read a poem that made us miss our mums,
Then I couldn't help but be glum,
When a stumpy bully made me feel sad
I tried to stand up for myself
But that just made him mad.

So I rushed to science, I tripped and fell,
I slipped; a horrible chemical,
Kids laughed at me and told me that I smelt,
They continued to point and mock
And during PE one of them stole my sock!

School is a place where I often sigh,
I won't let it get to me so I try not to cry.

Nowshin Ahmed

To My Mother

Mum, you laugh with me
even when laughing is the last thing
you want to be doing.
Matka, you take care of me when I'm
sick and lying in bed, even though you are
feeling so much worse than me.
Madre, you work long hours at work,
all for me to grow up and be the best person
I can be.
Ahm, you endure through all the pain and suffering
you have going on in your life, just so I can be
happy.
Mutter, you help me through this journey of
life, even though it is as foreign to you as it
is to me.
Nene, you continue to love me, even though
I have hurt and upset you countless times.
Majka, you're my lifeline, without you I would
be so lost.
Mare, you're my anchor, you ground me in
the best way possible.
Amma, I love you.

Mekha Benny

Loneliness

Thud!

The door slams and suddenly,
I'm left sullen and lonely,
There's nothing to watch or do,
The howling wind blew -

The curtains all over the room,
Instantly I wished the silence would resume,
Angry cars fly past the window,
I try to block out the noise with a pillow.

And, now, I've arrived at school,
With nowhere near enough fuel
To power me through the loneliness,
Even though I'm surrounded by people.

Behind all the smiles were the tears
And behind all the comfort were the fears,
Everything you think you see,
Wasn't everything there was to me.

Back at home, I'm now in bed,
Gazing at the stars to rest my head,
The ocean blues and light greys,
Everything I dream is in a haze.

Nathaniel Ebden (13)

To Live And Learn

To live is to learn and to learn is to live,
But when learning is controlled it's like we fall into an abyss,
Locked inside four prison walls, being told the same like rats being trained,
We fall into the abyss.
We live and we learn, we live and we learn.
A mantra spiralling down a slope, a slope we can escape?
Or is it a never-ending propaganda slope of shame?
Why should we cave? Why should we spiral?
We are the sun; no cloud will block us and no cloud ever could
Because we're always ready to shine when nobody
Ever thought we should.
So, stop what you're doing, take a look at your viewing
And breathe, for the next moment is yours.

Morgan Leah Critchley

Grade 9

"Grade 9!" the teacher cried
As they sat in neatly ordered lines,

Heads bowed they scribble,
Furiously,
Fearful eyes that turn towards
The clock's black hand
That slowly ticks towards.

"Learn the structure!" the teacher cried
As they sat in neatly ordered lines,

They exit the hall,
Grey tables left behind,
Nervous whispers exchanged.

"You must get the grades!" the teacher cried
As they sat in neatly ordered lines.

Trembling hands opening
Brown envelopes,
A set of numbers inside
That make or break
A future.

"Failure!" they cry,
Left behind by a broken system,
Where a 9 represents

Your ability to tread a certain path
But they leave in fractured lines.

Amelia Platt

My Life

Sometimes I feel
Like I'm in a prison cell,
I'm as free as a bird,
Yet I'm stuck in this hell.

The world goes on around me,
But I can't show myself,
They all see my act,
But the real me's on a shelf.

I try harder each day
To show them who I am,
Yet I'm still in my cage,
This is not what I am.

I might love drama,
I may love maths,
They can all call me lame,
But I can choose my path.

Tell you what,
I've had enough,
I'm more than just
A speck of dust.

Today's the day,
It'll be remembered forever,

I'll break free,
No matter the weather.

I won't stop now,
No, I won't back down,
This is my life
And I'll do it my way!

Vithoosha Chandirabalan (13)

Dear Future Me

Dear Future Me,
I know life has been tough
With a lot of stuff,
That was far from not being rough
Because I know for a fact it was a scruff,
But always remember you have people who care,
In your eyes it's rare,
But, in reality, everyone is there
For you, I swear.

Stick by the rules,
Don't break no hearts,
People have done you wrong,
But you're better than they could ever be,
Stick with the people who care
Because, I swear
It's worth it in the end.

Everyone knows friends come and go,
No need to suffer when one disappears,
Stay strong
And live life,
No matter what obstacles come in the way.

Dear Future Me,
Just be you

And it will all work out,
I promise.

Kainaat Tariq

Cyberbullying

I opened my eyes
To see what I had done,
Taking my final breath
As I descended into a never-ending dream.

This is how it started,
Also how it ended,
If only I was brave,
Brave is not an option for me.

If only people saw the real me,
Not the one I proclaimed to be,
Then maybe they would understand
I had been hit by too many bullets.

It all began one night,
Even though it was only one message
I cracked,
I couldn't survive another hit.

I had to do it,
It not like I wanted to,
But my heart was aching
From so many losses I had experienced.

My time had come to leave,
To leave the world I once enjoyed,

Maybe it was a joke,
But its effect was too painful to be said.

Nifemi Tijani

Smiling Society

Smile, breathe, count to ten,
Go back home,
Do it again,
Cry, drown, lose all will to live,
Can't drown these demons, they know how to swim.

Hide your sadness in this world of sin,
Because society doesn't *really* care about what is within.

Smile, breathe, make it through the day,
Because that's what we're taught, it's the only way,
Sadness, numbness, floods in your eyes,
People ask, "Are you okay?"
Drowning, you respond with "I'm fine."

Fat, ugly, battered, bruised,
Lost all sense of emotion,
I mean, *what have I got to lose?*

Smile, breathe, count to ten,
Welcome to society,
We hope you enjoy your stay.

Anna Kanthonga

When?

When will the sky be a little less grey?
When will the captains see their team is already great?
When will tutors praise students for turning up
Instead of punishing them for being late?
When will society tell me that I'm great?
When will elders listen to our cries?
When will mothers take their children with pride?
When will Parliament look upon the streets
To see the choices they made and the outcome it leaves?
When will the world look to the sea,
Revealing the damage of their plastic-covered meat?
When will the people finally listen to me,
The option I could give and the bright path that we could lead?

Mollie-Rose Smith

What Matters To Me?

What matters to me?
Can really be the most amazing thing that happened,
You will see,
I made a change in the world
In which I was hurled,
To #BeKind
In the heart and mind
And change people's way,
To help them say
Happy things,
They happily sing
Songs to embrace,
To embrace the difference
And flourish,
I have a different face you see,
To be myself and I is
What matters to me.
So, you see,
Embrace who you are,
You are a star
That shines all the time,
Say to yourself that everything will be fine,
Fine is okay,
Okay is fine,
This is what matters to me.

Nicholas Nikiforou (12)

Struggle

It's not how it seems,
As easy as can be,
Weird, but normal,
Assumptions from all,
What do I think?
Patience, embarrassment and struggle,
Noise can hurt him,
Words confuse him,
I can't always help him,
How do I feel?
Helpless, distressed, struggling,
The thoughts are different,
Perceptions of life as well,
How do I talk to him as others talk to their sibling?
Different, strangely and with struggle,
At the end of the day, I always say
The world is different without him,
Without all, with the disability,
Without it where would all inventions be?
Autism, be more aware.

Maria Aziz

A Girl Was Dancing To Life's Song

A girl was dancing
To life's sorrowful song,
It was a beautiful song,
But a sad, sad song.

The people had turned their backs,
Kept their eyes tight shut,
They didn't want to see
Her battle with the music.

And when she cried,
They walked away,
When she sobbed,
They closed their ears.

That lonely girl,
Now friendless and alone
And, yet, the song continues to play
And she continues to dance.

And if even one person watched,
The song would become more lively,
The girl would be happy.

So be that one person,
Don't let selfish desire cloud your heart,
Don't let ignorance rule you,

Write your own variation
Of life's song.

Melissa Faith Jones (15)

Just Let It Out

It burns like a fire
Yet it freezes like ice,
The feeling of wanting to speak,
But suffering the price.

I want to shout it out,
I want to scream,
"Spit it out!" they say,
"Stop living in a dream!"

My lips become numb,
Unable to move,
The room shrinks in
With nothing to prove.

They want me to talk,
Not knowing the truth
That escapes from my mouth,
Passing by each tooth.

Suddenly, the pain goes away,
I can speak once more,
I let it all out,
They look at me in disbelief
Of what they just saw.

Joseph Lewis Blakeley

The Jungle

The jungle reaches far and wide, with nowhere to hide,
Dangerous creatures wander in the night, waiting for people in sight,

The jungle reaches far and wide, with nowhere to hide,
The midnight sky passes by as all the creatures
say goodbye,

The jungle reaches far and wide, with nowhere to hide,
The wolves come out at night as it is the time to fright,

The jungle reaches far and wide, with nowhere to hide,
The clock strokes three and this usually scares me,
The jungle begins a riot and is no longer quiet,

All that's left to do is say goodbye to you,
You may be astonished, but I guarantee I am honest.

Emma Skinner (11)

I Will Shout

I may be small but my words are not,
They are wildfires, burning down cities in a manner
of minutes,
Earthquakes that shake,
Hearts that break,
Tools that make,
My words are powerful.

Soaring through pitch-black nights,
They fly on winds to the ears of beggars and kings,
They are nothing
And
Everything,
My words are deeper than the deepest ocean,
Darker than the darkest night,
My words are my greatest weapon,

And I will not be quiet.

I will shout,
I will scream,
I will make so much noise you won't be able to ignore me,
I may be small but my words are not,
And I will not stop until I am heard.

India-Rose Marriott (17)

Call Me Cynical

Weddings are funerals,
The death of freedom
And submission to love,
Like the hopeless flight
Of a wingless dove.

I do,
I don't
Because if I will,
You won't,
Love is dangerous if it isn't returned,
It maims and causes the heat to rise.

The fires of hell
Burn her white dress,
Charring it black,
While the light of heaven
Burns his heart,
They stay together 'til death do us part
And tear each other to pieces.

Oh, we're all mad here my dear friend,
Right to our miserable end,
But the money will allow her to buy her shoes
To wear to your cremation
And make her finally care and pay attention.

Lauren Rose Schofield (15)

Ellen

A response to 'The Farmer's Bride' by Charlotte Mew

Finally, behind the bushes, I hide,
Twigs dashed across my eyes,
Exposing my naked whites through the cracks of thorny knives,
Leaves scattered like broken, emerald glass,
My breath is heavier than the air,
But I couldn't see him near,
Flashes of yellow, amber and brown
Taunt me, like wood burning in fire.
Branches surround and consume me
Like veins around my beating heart.

My blood pulsating,
I can hear dogs running,
Running,
Yelling,
Shouting,
Barking.

Amber, that torches show, flashes in my pupils
As heat prickles my skin and as I hide my eyes,
They have found me! They found me!

Ifeoluwa Olusolape Afuwape (17)

Who Said Love Had To Be Soft?

Who said love had to be soft?
It's true,
I am not guilty of needing you
Like those hopelessly romantic,
Yet, I crave you, inside and out,
I yearn for the ease you bring to my smile,
I hunger for your acid touch,
For our bodies to lay on a canvas and pray for art.
I thirst for the days I remember the warmth of your kisses,
The bitterness in your piercing tears
And the joy in your gleaming eyes.
I seek for you to bloom with me,
Wildly, ferociously, boldly,
I beg for you to call me, hurricane,
For you to root for our untamed love.

Judit Climent (17)

Betrayal

You said that you cared for me,
That we were friends, you would always be there,
You said you would never leave, and that part I actually believed,
But you slowly lost interest,
Slowly stopped to care,
Slowly stopped to notice that I was even there.
First, you left me broken, drowning in despair,
Then you left me thinking, were you never really there?
Never really by my side,
Never looking back,
Never really did you care,
'Cause you stabbed me in the back.
They say to watch out for your enemy,
Ones whose hearts are full of jealousy,
But, in the end,
I was hurt by the one I called my friend.

Dina Samha (12)

Grandad

I know that I will see you again,
But I am not sure when
I'll hear your voice
And realised that it was the best choice,
But now, I miss you, we all do.

When I see you again,
It will all be new,
You will see how much we grew,
For now, I will always love you
And I know that you love me too!

The memories we have had will never fade,
For when beautiful flowers are laid
Our faces will smile, yours too
Because the love that we have for you is true.

Grandad, you were the best,
Without you, I cannot rest
I know that you would tell me to grin
Because Heaven for me and you is a great thing!

Amy Turner

My Truth

My truth
Is hidden to all,
Closed from all,
Separated from all.

My truth
Is dark and deep,
Dangerous from me,
Deadly for you.

My truth
Is that I am dark,
I am the voice in your head,
I am the scars on your arms.

My truth
Is that I am the monster under the bed,
I am the nightmares you have,
I am the suicide you attempt.

My truth
Is that some call me the black dog,
Some call me the black hole,
Some call me a curse.

My truth
Is that I am a liar,

I am your friend,
I am your enemy.

My truth
Is all of these things,
But above all
My truth
Is that I am depression
And I must be fought.

Elizabeth-Leigh Vogel-Stevens

The Abyss

I was falling, falling,
I was screaming, screaming,
I was crying, crying,
I was bleeding, bleeding.

I was falling through the abyss,
Falling, falling,
I was screaming through the abyss,
Screaming, screaming,
I was crying through the abyss,
Crying, crying,
I was bleeding through the abyss,
Bleeding, bleeding,
I was to die in the abyss, on my way to hell,

I saw openings from the human world,
I saw a sword, famously named Excalibur,
I saw chances flashing by,
I saw and I grabbed one, so I didn't die.

I was flung through the air into a portal of light,
I knew that this was my fight.

Evelyn Grace Boyd (12)

Nature's Warning

Destructive and vicious is the rain,
Falling and gathering in large amounts,
Quickly turning to floods, snatching homes,
Isn't it obvious Mother Earth is in pain?

There are orange crisp flames,
Burning trees, reducing oxygen,
Encouraged by the wind and enraged at us,
Spreading violently, untamed.

Winds howl, the ground rumbles and shakes,
Cracks destroy the smooth surface,
Tremors break the peace,
Swallowing buildings in their wake.

Clocks tick louder, almost faster,
All these signs must be a warning,
Last chance at a wake-up call,
We are suffering from global warming.

Aysha Mahmood (12)

Wrongdoings

Sometimes, I wonder, while gazing into space,
Why people feel inclined to be horrid?
In my case, it's immature, wrong, there's no need to hurt,
Are you hurt inside?
Let us help you recover
The things that click in their broken brains
That seem normal to them, but to us, insane,
They kill and steal and do witless things,
I don't understand them, I think it's inane,
Then again, to themselves, it's probably fine,
Maybe they'll realise, just maybe in time,
It seems such a waste of a human life,
Are you hurt inside?
Let us help you recover.

Max Coxon (12)

Be Quick, Swift And Silent Boy

Quickly, quickly,
Too brave to speak,
Try and claw your way up to their peaks,
The icy gaze of a hero's from home
Will light the fire inside your own,
Clouds can rise, but speed will win.
Falling into the trap of beasts been bitten.

Swiftly, swiftly,
Bare your claws,
For the dogs must do a tiger's chore,
Their wounds will heal, but never will yours
Because the world is too small
To fit a heart like yours.

Silence, silence,
Echoes in your ears,
As you watched your life being torn to fear,
A sacrifice you did make for
The price to raise a lion's roar.

Elizabeth Rose Price (12)

Little Mr Raindrop

Little Mr Raindrop, why do you fall?
Little Mr Raindrop, why must you die?
Little Mr Raindrop, why don't you call?
Little Mr Raindrop, please don't cry,
Little Mr Raindrop, please do not leave,
Little Mr Raindrop, you are so young,
Little Mr Raindrop, we will all grieve,
Little Mr Raindrop, talents unsung,
Little Mr Raindrop, didn't fit in,
Little Mr Raindrop, it's so unfair,
Little Mr Raindrop, just couldn't win,
Little Mr Raindrop, seen as just air,
Little Mr Raindrop, forced from the crowd,
So, Mr Raindrop, you jumped from the cloud.

Rhys Yeaxlee (14)

Colours

Will you paint me in colour?
Draw me into your sunflower,
A mix of tones that are golden,
Glistening golds that pull you in.
Write me a love note
On yellow paper, sealed with hope,
Make me bright again,
Though I wish not to be a rainbow,
I hope not to be put on show,
No.
I want to be the sun.
A shining ball
That brings light to all,
Those around me, let the warmth from my rays
Keep you safe for all your days.

I want you to paint me in yellow
So that I will never again feel this low.
I want you to paint me in yellow
And never let me go.

Macy Ann Hall (17)

If Life Was A Game...

Pitfalls, turmoil, life and death,
Pain and love with every breath,
Spirits broken, lessons learnt,
Limits vanished, peace earnt,
A fierce beauty beneath that look,
Another chapter closed in that book,
Pain beneath laughter, tears beneath smiles,
Every day, brave soldiers travel miles,
Struggling, striving, hidden in plain sight,
Most chapters of their stories concealed within the night,
Strength beyond imagination,
New sets of smiles for every occasion,
Fresh battle scars on young hearts,
If life was a game, they'd have the most marks.

Fatima Mohiuddin (12)

What Will Happen?

What will happen
When the air blackens?
When the sea comes crashin'
Like the Kraken?

Or when the land
Goes bland
And the beach and the sand
Are no more than a dreamland?

Or when Man uses their 'high throne'
And accidentally breaks the layer of ozone?
It would be so hot, a bone
Would melt, unlike stone.

Or when a creature, such as a crow,
The amount of them drops very low?
Fast approaching zero,
Earth will need a hero.

Alfie Fitzgerald

Stay

I wish I could keep you
For one more lifetime,
I wish I didn't come to the place we met
So late,
Maybe, then
This departure,
This terrible departure
Wouldn't hurt as much as it does now.

Do I describe you as my beacon?
Yes.
Do I love you too much?
Yes.
Did I admire how
When I felt like I was drowning,
Your smile was the only thing that kept me from falling?
Even though I knew that the world around you
Was colliding and exploding?
Yes.

Ayomide Adesesan

Alone

It started just a few nights,
Then a lot of nights
And then she was never home.

I missed my parents' marriage.

My dad tried to help me,
To console me,
To protect me.

But it was never going to work.

I am not an imbecile,
I know this ill-placed guilt
Will try to kill my dad,

In more ways than one.

But I will be ready
And I will be strong,
I will save my dad from his strife,

So I will not be alone.

Izzy Goldberg (11)

You Thought You Were Free

You fell into the light,
In the darkness of the night,
Cried out with your fright.
Your soul was on fire,
You cried out with desire,
You thought you were free.

You stood up on two legs,
Found time to recollect,
Looked up to the sky
And realised how high,
You thought you were free.

You began to be bold,
New habits turned to old,
Tried to grab a hold,
You thought you were free.

You grew to mature,
Started to endure,
You thought you were free.

Your wizened face smiled,
You thought you were free.

Now you are free.

Megan Josephine Swanson (14)

The Door Of Success

Knock, knock, knocking
while the people behind are mocking.
Knock, knock, stopping,
the people behind are blocking.

Blocking with their downgrading words
that fly into her soul like thunderbirds,
Thunderbirds with no thunder,
but still, they strike her asunder.

Hopelessness will become hope,
less you lie around and mope.
Make your way back to me,
you are but a step away from your glee.

Knock, knock, knocking,
the people behind are mocking.
Knock, knock, opening...
Success says, "Welcome in."

Ifeoluwa Ayeni (13)

Shattering

His eyes held secrets that would never touch his lips,
They held a darkness that was daunting,
A fire that was spreading,
Waves which came crashing.

Her eyes held secrets that would never touch her lips,
They held glass that was cracking,
A hurricane and tornado clashing,
Tides which came crashing.

Their fights were like a storm,
Their happiness was like a tsunami,
Their sadness was like a volcanic eruption,
But their love...

Their love was the whole Earth shattering.

Samia Roshid

Sadness And Love

Sad, happy, my feelings are wacky,
When all if down, I try to be happy,
Surprise and shock filed in a box.

Love is complicated, but yet it lasts long,
I'm trying to look, but I can't find you,
Time and time until butterflies fly,
I knew that I had found you.

As I run in black, I feel blank,
Sadness has taken me, I feel grey.
As the years go by, I feel lost
With no one to love before the timer ends.

Sara Syposz

Free Time

The school bell has chimed,
I have some free time!
What shall I do?
What would you do?
I could...
Read a book,
Or have a look
At the amusing photos
That I took.

Dancing isn't bad
And I'm very glad to add
Swimming in the local pool,
In the water clear and cool.

Flip, flop!
Drip, drop!

Whoopeee!
This is the life for meee!

2016.

Sophia Georgina Verai (12)

Some Rules Are Meant To Be Broken

Why must we always abide by rules?
Rules which society lays out for us,
They are like barriers,
Walls fixing us onto a set path,
There is no freedom, there are no choices,
The rules state that we must look like this,
Act in a particular way,
You must be this size, this height,
This colour hair and this colour eyes,
But what if we broke free?
Be who we wanted to be?
Discarded each stereotype?
Burned each judgement?
What if I started being me?

Sophie Bagley (14)

Forever

His body, a fast tsunami,
I'm caught in the tides,
Flames dancing in his eyes,
I caught his stifling fire,
His words a forever black hole,
I'm lost in the welcoming darkness,
I'm staring at his grey facade,
Brown eyes penetrating my ones,
I'm lost,
I'm found,
I'm knowledgable,
I'm confused,
I am his,
He is mine,
My world is no longer hazy.

Anna Golding

These Days And Clichés

This is how kids are raised,
We're praised
For not eating for days,
All stuck in that phase,
Thinking our bodies are displays,
Make-up painted on our face,
Thinking of another way
To make us look better than yesterday,
We delay our grades and essays
Cos being dumb is the new craze,
I'm dying to go back
To the old days,
The clichés,
You ever heard of the phrase
I miss the good old days?
I miss the good old days.

Deanna Watson (15)

A Universe Inside Her Mind

A repetitive echo of taps start up,
The scintillating screen a cutting edge in the darkness.
This.
This is her safe haven
And as worlds begin tumbling from her fingers,
As a universe unravels from her mind,
Her life seems brighter than ever,
Especially as the sun starts to send shadows across every surface,
Every trace of a saturnine mood dissipates
As she falls, falls, falls into the storybook world
And she never stops falling.

Madeleine Palash-Weeks

Lies

What used to seem cool,
Making me feel like a fool,
Causing me to hide,
Too scared to shine,
Everything you owned was mine,
But I gave it to you with an open mind,
I looked at you with a smile,
But thought otherwise in a while,
You took me by surprise
When you said "Goodbye,"
When I asked why, you left me with a random lie,
But today, here I stand with pride,
So pleased that I have moved on,
Well, at least I tried.

Sumaia Rahimi (12)

When Is It Home Time?

Pens, pencils, rulers,
I am all equipped for school,
I would rather be at home though,
Just sitting in my room.

English, maths, geography,
How boring can it be?
I would rather be at home though,
Just watching the TV.

Grab your bags, coats and books,
It's time to leave the day behind,
Oh, what a day it's been,
Thank god it's home time!

Grace Robinson (13)

Teardrop

All I smell
Is the scent of my sorrow,
Burning a hole through my heart
Like a fiery arrow.

Can you hear me
When I shout your name?
Can you see me
While you're bathing in fame?

I ran in the pouring rain,
Dripping from my hair,
Knocked on your door
To find you weren't there.

Walking back,
My heart slowly dying,
I hear your laugh,
But why am I crying?

Aimee Dalby (11)

Silent Voices

Unshackle these bonds of silence,
Let us rise like the break of dawn,
From the depths of loss, hope and solitude
May we find our voices.

The world may see our spark,
But we must feel it.

Set this life on fire,
Run dry these emotions
'Til we fall with the nations and
Become one with dusk.

Never find comfort in silence,
Or your story won't be heard.

Shenelle Davis

I Am More Than You See

I am not my face,
I am not my hair,
I am not the uniform
You see me wear,
I am not my skin,
I am not my smile,
You'll see who I am
If you sit and talk a while,
I like what I see
When I look to the skies,
There is more to me,
Than what meets the eye,
I'm tired of always being
Unfairly judged,
I am who I am
And on that, I won't budge.

Paris Christina Branch

Emotions

Silence is an emotion,
Life stops.
No sudden motion,
A piece of soothing music, then the beat drops.

Happiness is a part of life,
Positive vibes saunter round.
Depression is a sharp knife,
Positive vibes don't make a sound.
Nerves are always blatant,
And crawl into your mind.
They are triggered and not very patient,
And not difficult to find...

Dylan Singh Bains (11)

The Shadow

I could see a shadow
Quite far away,
I was speechless,
I didn't know what to say.

It moved swiftly,
Leaving a trail of mist,
It seemed like a ghost,
But with a twist.

It had no face,
Just a round head,
It tried to grab me
But its hand just fell through my wrist instead.

Lewis Paul Healey (12)

Lost

I'm lost in the darkness
Of the world,
Lost.
I'm lost in the middle of nowhere,
Lost.
I'm lost in the memories
Of the deserted past,
Lost.
I'm lost in reality.

Lost,
On the surface of the Earth,
Silence is everywhere,
Time is spinning, life is to an end.

Skeena Zara Shah (11)

To Whom It May Concern

To you whom I despise
And yet love so dearly.

To you who took everything
And yet nothing at all.

To you whose life means so little
And yet so much to me.

To you who cared so little
And yet I cared so much.

To you who broke me down
And yet managed to make me stronger.

My emotional instability,
My father.

I owe it all to you.

Megan Healan (17)

A House On A Hill

A house on a hill, through storms and disaster still stands,
Broken windows, locked doors, trapped in the house,
Floods and fires, droughts and famine,
Only the strongest survive,
Heartache, loss and pain,
Trapped forever,
No hope of rescue,
Only a long war,
A long wait,
So long
And no saviour awaits.

Anna Hale

Epiphany

I'd come to realise that it was not me looking in,
Nor them looking out,
But us all looking, searching, trying to understand what each other was looking at,
Past our mirrors of hate and lies
Lies a truer reflection of jumbled words and phrases that make up the entirety of...
You.

Ruth Adetunji (15)

The Secret Word

Imagine a wonderful world
Free of crime and poverty,
Envision a place
Full of grace,
Using your creative ability
You can invent stability,
Visit places full of tranquillity
And go beyond your wildest dreams,
We all have one,
Big or small
But what am I?
I am your imagination

Jelani Cecil Eguakun (14)

Phones Are Bad

Keep them away!
They're killers, they rot your brain!
Take your life, take your name,
Give you cancer,
They don't even care
That it can leave you with no hair,
Get out of that screen,
Go outside,
Think more green.

Guinevere Sophronia Edith Fiske (11)

Glass Ceilings

A ballerina looks at the glass world
eager to dance her way
through the ceilings

she cracks her feet
and glares at her shattered reflections

the shards scream

her feet patter, and repeat.

Tiyana Lashae Robinson Henriques (18)

I Love You

You are the one
Of all times,
The stars always shine on you,
I love you,
You are the one
Of all times,
You will always be with me,
I love you,
I love you.

Emily Jane Carmel Roberts

Young Writers Information

We hope you have enjoyed reading this book – and that you will continue to in the coming years.

If you're a young writer who enjoys reading and creative writing, or the parent of an enthusiastic poet or story writer, do visit our website **www.youngwriters.co.uk**. Here you will find free competitions, workshops and games, as well as recommended reads, a poetry glossary and our blog. There's lots to keep budding writers motivated to write!

If you would like to order further copies of this book, or any of our other titles, then please give us a call or visit **www.youngwriters.co.uk**.

Young Writers
Remus House
Coltsfoot Drive
Peterborough
PE2 9BF
(01733) 890066
info@youngwriters.co.uk

Join in the conversation!
Tips, news, giveaways and much more!

YoungWritersUK   **@YoungWritersCW**